© 2006 by Helen Exley Giftbooks

Selection and arrangement © 2006 Helen Exley
Copyright © Yoneo Morita 2006, Licensed by Intercontinental Licensing
The moral right of the author has been asserted.

Written by Pam Brown © 2006 Helen Exley

This 2006 edition published by Barnes & Noble, Inc.
by arrangement with Exley Publications, Ltd.

ISBN-13: 978-0-7607-8900-1
ISBN-10: 0-7607-8900-2

Printed and bound in China

10 9 8 7 6 5 4 3 2 1

Cuddly cats

BY PAM BROWN

BARNES & NOBLE

NEW YORK

Dear cats. Dear best

of friends.

How small a creature
to hold one's heart.

It doesn't matter

if you are six feet four

and broad of shoulder,

if a kitten is looking for

a mother-figure

—you're it.

She has no words

She has no words, but by small touchings

and buttings,

she shows

her love for you

and tries to distract you from your sorrow.

so small

So small a creature

to make so

great a difference

to your life.

Kit, Katten,   Cat. Ch

Kit, Katten, Cat. Charm. Mischief. Wisdom.

One never ceases to find
new wonders in a cat.
Pattern and swirl of fur, elegance of movement,
perfection of form.
Delicacy of whisker, brilliance of eye,
gentleness of outstretched paw
and loving, butting head. Expressiveness of tail.
Complexity of ear.
A mouth of pink and ivory, curved tongue
and shining teeth.
A voice of mystery.

poise, grace

We seek beauty, poise, grace, elegance.
The cat does not.
He has them already.

elegance

all beautiful

There are quiet, shy, gentle kittens,

and comic, bold as brass kittens.

And all beautiful.

And all needing a human being who will think them

the very best kitten in the universe.

purr rurr ur

...his purr overflows
his heart
to fill the room.

I don't think the word "relax"
was invented until
the discovery of The Cat.

Round, misty-blue eyes stare desperately. Love me, they say, let me into your life, so that I can begin to take over your entire existence.

misty-blue

eyes

Cats don't see why
they should waste time
learning words.
After all—they have no intention
of obeying anyone.

utterly supe

o r

Cat has always known

his lineage was more distinguished

than any Pharoah.

And has lived his life accordingly.

A cat is always
on the wrong side of any door.

After scolding one's cat
one looks into its face
and is seized
by the ugly suspicion
that it understood
every word.
And has filed it
for reference.

Any cat can look at
any disaster and say,
"It wasn't me,"
with a perfectly
straight face.

"It wasn't

me."

The smallest kitten
only needs a week
to be in full possession
of a house
and its owners.

the boss

the

Cats, you must

realize, have quietly

taken over the world.

real rulers

A cat lies
where he wants to lie.

A small cat stretches out
its paw
to touch your face
—and you are no longer
lost or lonely.

So small—so full of love

and ingenuity.

So frail—so full of life.

stillness

Cat says:

Now is the time for stillness.

Caress my fur and I will sing for you.

And my song will soothe your heart

to quietness.

warmth

When the heart
is desolate a little cat
will warm
and comfort it.

and comfort

CAT CLAWS

Cat's claws were given to it to hunt,
to fight, and to climb trees,
but centuries have extended its abilities
to shin up curtains,
open doors, lift lids, and rearrange
the ornaments.

No cat is as virtuous as he looks.

little
devil

A kitten brings a joy
out of all proportion
to its size.

she brings

joy

A cat does not speculate
about its future.
It does not analyze its past.
It has no ambitions or regrets.
It accepts the moment and makes
the best of it.

A cat is, in the eyes of the doctors,
a splendid calming device,
an aid to a healthy heart.
True. If he hasn't tripped you on the stair
or leapt from the darkness, unexpectedly,
eyes glowing, claws grappling your neck.
In sheer affection.

Buy in bulk
the food your cat adores—
and be withered
with contempt.

To be cut dead by one's cat
means one has committed a heinous sin.
Words won't rectify the matter.
Shrimps may.

totally

A cat expects to be adored.

All kittens set out

to teach their humans to adapt

to the needs of a cat.

As a reward,

they grant them the position

of honorary cat.

teacher o

humans

A cat can explain exactly what he wants without a single word.

"Behind the ears now. Now the fluffy bit along the jawbone. And now the chin and throat. (Yes, smooth my whiskers, but don't overdo it.) A gentle rubbing of the teeth. The chest now. And now, best and most beautiful, my glorious belly— stretched out for you to scratch. A good all over smoothing and we can sleep."

little cat

How comforting
the gentle snoring
of a little cat.

A sulking cat is solid sulk.

Human beings are drawn to cats
because they are all we are not
   —self-contained, elegant in everything
they do, relaxed, assured.

coming home

One small cat
changes coming home
to an empty house
to coming home.

A cat loves
to help you
tidy your papers.

a tummy rub please

He is a kindly cat, loving beyond reason;

head-butter, nuzzler, flubsy sprawl of fur,

belly spread, he lies like an upturned table,

forepaws kneading, demanding notice

and a tummy rub.

superior species

Cats know, quietly and with
complete conviction,
that they are the superior species.

A cat believes

in privacy.

His. Not yours.

A cat will vividly enact

the chase with a dry leaf

    as a mouse—until some silly human

being says,

    "Kill it. Kill the mouse!"

    When he will stare in disdain,

"Mouse? for heaven's sake, can't you see

    it's a dead leaf!"

One has a quite exceptionally clever and conversational cat—and one tells one's friends. They come to call—and are confronted by an animal who appears to be not entirely right in the head. It stares at them blankly. "Me? I'm just a poor stupid pussycat." And goes away to laugh in some quiet corner.

Do not confuse the implements
in your cat's feet with simple claws.
They are excavators, stilettos,
slings, lancets, rippers of curtains, engravers
of furniture.

m y s t i f

A cat is mystified when you don't understand his perfectly clear conversation.

People, in exasperation,

sometimes wonder whether they own their cats,

or their cats own them.

The cats do not need to speculate.

who?

Dizwiz plays at being dead
when she is called.
And smiles knowing each eccentricity
makes us love her all the more.

Any cat knows the precise
cost of every
form of cat food
and chooses, unfailingly,
the most expensive.

e s

calling the cat

You have been calling the cat

for twenty minutes.

He is sitting three yards from you

in the shelter of a bush. Amused.

A cat will share
your bed—just as long
as you don't fidget
or breathe
too heavily.

Cats appear to be behaving impeccably.
Until you explore the hidden places.
The curtain linings—in shreds.
The sofa back—in ribbons.
The wallpaper behind the door—gouged.
The carpet in the hall—tufted.
The potted plant—stunted.
Corner the culprit and be met with reproach.
"Me?"

A cat could talk
if he wanted to.
But he doesn't.

indifference

Cat owners sometimes have an ugly suspicion that the Lord of the Universe has whiskers and a long, ginger tail.

Joy is to see
a little lost cat
ambling up
the garden path.

little
lost one

The gentle
touch of an
outstretched paw.
The butt
of a head.
The trust
and affection
of a little cat.

A gentle touch

Cats bring
the scent of summer
home on their fur.

the scent
of summer

There is nothing so asleep as a kitten.

...gentle
sleep

It's a hard heart
a kitten
cannot melt.

melts your he

art

disa

In mid chase
she stops. Sits. Washes her feet.
Stares at you with disapproval.
"For heaven's sake woman,"
she declares.
"Act your age."

proval

A cat will show its

outer beauty to the world

and perhaps hint at

its affectionate heart.

All else is hidden—

kept for the one it loves.

for the one it

oves

My cat and I
are growing old together.
We love sleep and food
and watching
the world go by.

Old ladies, after a lifetime

of dealing with people, find the company

of cats a great relief.

Cats being companionable and kind, courteous

in their dictatorial demands, delicate

in their greed, clean, beautiful, and elegant…

And vulnerable as we all are.

a lifet

me

the stuff of d

Cats lend us
magic and the stuff
of dreams.

eams

The pleasure
of living with a cat
is that you never
discover
all its secrets.

No wonder I like cats.
They are far more simple,
but so much better at being cats
than we are
at being human.

We hold every cat
that we have ever had
safe in our
hearts
forever.

The team that created *Cuddly Cats*

PAM BROWN THE AUTHOR

For over twenty years, Pam Brown has been writing
for Helen Exley Giftbooks. Her subjects have included
family relationships, wisdom, and cats.
Her best writing is reserved for the subjects near to her heart,
and distilled from her knowledge and observation.
The cats Pam writes about have been her friends—
Henry, Gandalf, Charlie, Albert, Tiggy, Duplicat, Buster, Bundle—
plus various passing strangers—all of them rugged individuals.
Pam Brown recently moved to Devon, England with present,
infinitely inventive cat, Vincent. She is rediscovering
the pleasures of gardening, country food, and clear bright air
with a view of the moors. She has a son, two daughters,
and a vast array of grandchildren nearby.

SHE DEDICATES THIS BOOK:

*To Vincent and the cats of the world—each a mystery,
each a link into the wilderness.*

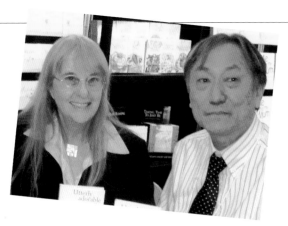

YONEO MORITA THE PHOTOGRAPHER

Yoneo Morita, who took the stunning photographs in the book,
was born in Ito, Japan in 1950. He graduated in photography in Tokyo,
and after working in a photographic library, has spent
more than a decade capturing thousands of people's pets on camera.
He adores cats (he and his wife have twenty cats and six dogs
in their own home), and has the patience—sometimes taking
a week or more—to gain the friendship and acceptance
of all his "models." This enables him to get the humorous, trusting,
and intimate "fish-eye" shots that have become his trademark.
Yoneo Morita's work, with its familiar Hanadeka
("big nose") emblem, is now licensed to publishers and manufacturers
in more than twenty countries around the world.